a gift of
awakening

a gift of
awakening

Gill Farrer-Halls
With illustrations from the
collection of Robert Beer

Andrews McMeel
Publishing
Kansas City

First published by MQ Publications Limited
12 The Ivories, 6–8 Northampton Street
London, N1 2HY

Copyright © 2004 MQ Publications Limited
Text © 2004 Gill Farrer-Halls
Illustrations © 2004 Robert Beer

Series editor: Abi Rowsell
Design: Yvonne Dedman

ISBN: 0-7407-4064-4

Library of Congress Control Number: 2003113050
03 04 05 06 07 PAR 10 9 8 7 6 5 4 3 2 1

Attention: Schools and Businesses
Andrews McMeel books are available at quantity discounts with bulk purchase for educational, business, or sales promotional use. For information, please write to: Special Sales Department, Andrews McMeel Publishing, 4520 Main Street, Kansas City, Missouri 64111.

contents

introduction

The Sanskrit word *karma* is now part of the English language. Expressions such as "bad karma" and "good karma" are commonly used these days. Jokes such as "Your karma ran over my dogma" are amusing but don't make sense, and expose the fact that most of us native English speakers do not have much understanding of the true meaning of the word. We tend to use this term to describe a mystical fate or fortune, which is not entirely incorrect but does miss the full meaning and subtle complexities of what karma is and how it works in our lives. This book takes a look at what karma really means.

Firstly, note that the original texts of Buddhism were written in Sanskrit and Pali. Karma is called "kamma" in Pali, the Indic language used in the canonical books of Buddhism. You will see both versions in the quotations used in this book, but they mean the same thing.

The law of karma

Sometimes people refer to the law of karma as a natural and inescapable law of the universe. While integral to Buddhist teachings, including those about compassion and wisdom, essentially karma means action, although this is a general definition.

More precisely, Buddhists say that karma refers to actions that are willed or meant—that is, those that have intention behind them. However, even if we do something instinctively, without thinking about it, there is still some level of unconscious intention at work.

Therefore, all of our actions can create karma. Their effects can vary between being powerful or weak depending on different conditions and situations. Traditional Buddhist texts state that Buddhas, or people who have become enlightened, are the only ones whose actions are perfectly "pure" and no longer generate any karma.

Mental, verbal, and bodily karma

Karma has a threefold classification:

1. mental karma—created by the mind and thoughts,
2. verbal karma—created by speech, and
3. bodily karma—caused by physical actions.

Mental karma is the most significant of the three because it gives rise to, and is the origin of, the other two types of karma. We think before we speak or physically do something, however briefly, and our thoughts influence what we say and do.

Furthermore, two types of karmic actions are described here: ones that are positive, skillful, beneficial, and also good, and those that are negative, unskillful, harmful, and ultimately bad.

Ten negative actions that create bad karma

There are ten main negative actions that create bad karma: the three physical acts of killing, stealing, and sexual misconduct (including acts such as adultery); followed by the four negative acts of speech, i.e., lying, saying things to harm others or cause conflict between them, using harsh language such as swearing, and idle gossip; and ending with the three mental negative acts of covetousness, thinking ill of people, and holding wrong views, such as not understanding that anger causes suffering.

Ten positive actions that create good karma

These involve, first, giving up all negative actions, as noted before, and then cultivating their positive opposites. The three physical virtues are protecting life, being generous to others, and responsible sexual behavior. The four positive acts of speech include being truthful, creating harmony and reconciliation among others, talking pleasantly, and having useful conversations. The three mental virtues are being content with what one has, being kind to others, and developing conviction that what the Buddha taught is beneficial.

Negative karma

Negative karma arises from actions that are driven by ignorance or delusion; hatred, aversion, or anger; or greed, attachment, or avarice. These are called the Three Poisons in Buddhism, and are the qualities that keep us trapped in samsara, the cycle of birth and rebirth, which we only escape by reaching enlightenment.

Positive karma

Positive karma arises from actions that are not rooted in ignorance, hatred, or greed. Although we could say positive karma arises from wisdom, love, and renunciation, it is traditional to describe the positive qualities as directly opposite to the Three Poisons, because this reminds us of what they are and to try to avoid them.

Three stages must occur for an action to be complete:

1. the motivation to perform the action,
2. the successful fulfillment of the action, and
3. the satisfaction of completing the action.

If only one or two stages are fulfilled, the karma created is less, while a completed action generates greater karmic consequences. For example, if you mistakenly squash an insect and are sorry to have killed it, only the action itself has occurred; there was no intention or satisfaction in the act.

The karmic consequences are, therefore, less than if you deliberately jumped on the insect and were happy to have successfully killed it.

The law of cause and effect

Karma is also called the law of cause and effect. This means that every action, however tiny or seemingly insignificant, creates a cause for an eventual result, which is called the fruit of the action. These consequences are complex and influenced by hundreds of little factors during our lives, and through many different lifetimes, that intermingle. Because of this, we often cannot see clearly how karma operates.

Karmic fruition may be
experienced in this lifetime,
in the next lifetime,
or in other, future lives.

Karmic fruition

Most human actions create karmic consequences that are not experienced immediately but will definitely be experienced later.

The Buddhist scriptures say that the majority of our actions will bear fruit in future lives. A kind, generous, honest person who suffers in this life can rest assured he or she will experience the positive karmic consequences of his or her good actions in a later life. Someone behaving in ways that cause suffering for others, but enjoying a happy life, will suffer the consequences of the negative behavior in a later life.

Karma and rebirth

Karma and rebirth are deeply interlinked. What exactly is rebirth? Buddhism considers that only our most subtle consciousness goes from one life to the next. The individual person, both personality and characteristics, is extinguished at death. This subtle consciousness carries with it all the karma created in the life just finished, together with any karma from previous lives that has not yet come to fruition. These karmic imprints determine the quality of the next life, while some of the karma carried over will also come to fruition in the next life when it meets the appropriate conditions.

Certain behavior creates specific karmic consequences

A person who easily finds prosperity in this life may have created the cause by being generous in a previous existence. Someone who dies young in this life might have failed to protect others in a previous life.

Beauty could be the result of pure, ethical behavior in a past life, while people who are not taken seriously in this life may have created the cause by lying in a past existence. These examples illustrate how karma is linked with ethical, responsible behavior—we reap what we sow.

Black and white

Karma is classified according to its results. The first category is called

- **black** karma, **black** result

and includes all harmful actions of body, speech, and mind.

- white karma, white result

incorporates all nonharmful and virtuous actions.

- **black** and white karma,

  black and white result

includes actions that are partly harmful, partly not. For example, telling a lie in order not to hurt someone's feelings. Although the intention is positive, the act itself is not, so the karmic consequences will be mixed.

The last category needs more explanation. This is:

- karma that is neither **black** nor white, a result that is neither **black** nor white.

This arises when our underlying intention is to transcend the other kinds of karma altogether by trying to become enlightened, the ultimate goal of Buddhism. The purpose of practicing Buddhism is to avoid suffering and find happiness. This may make us feel that creating karma that brings happiness as the result is the best thing to do.

However, Buddhism teaches us that everything is impermanent, so even if we create the causes of happiness, the resulting happiness cannot last forever. Sooner or later the karma that created happiness will be exhausted and we will experience suffering. Our highest aspiration is to transcend karma on our path toward enlightenment.

Rebirth

While some early Christian sects believed in a form of rebirth, it is quite a difficult concept for some Westerners to accommodate. Since people are born with certain talents, however, we can begin to understand how karma moves from one life to the next. People with outstanding musical talent, for example, often speak of how they felt as if they already knew how to play music when they first started. Similarly, Mozart learned how to play music very quickly at an early age and had an inner sense of harmony and rhythm.

The Noble Eightfold Path

Attaining enlightenment is not easy! It is a state in which one is completely free from desire for, and attachment to, things one likes, and also from aversion to, and hatred for, what one doesn't like.

To develop the conditions within which this state may arise, Buddhists follow the Buddha's Noble Eightfold Path, which is a guide to living in a manner that does not cause suffering to oneself or others. It was created to help people reach enlightenment.

Enlightenment is the total liberation from suffering that the Buddha discovered, also referred to as nirvana and awakening.

This explanation of karma makes one thing very clear:

> we are responsible for
> whatever occurs in our lives.

The Noble Eightfold Path

The Noble Eightfold Path comprises:
1. Right view
2. Right thought
3. Right speech
4. Right action
5. Right livelihood
6. Right effort
7. Right mindfulness
8. Right concentration

The person who has happiness, health, and success created the foundations for a pleasant life by performing positive actions in previous lives.

Those who suffer illness, poverty, and so forth, likewise created the causes for their unpleasant experiences by committing negative actions previously. Most people have a mixture of good and bad experiences throughout their lives, reflecting the varied karma they created in earlier lives. So, karma is not fatalistic. By consciously trying to act with wisdom, love, kindness, and compassion for others as much as possible, we create the karma for positive rebirths. Virtuous behavior will eventually lead us beyond karma altogether, to enlightenment.

Purification

So, can anything be done about all the negative karma that has been created over many different lifetimes? Obviously it would be preferable not to experience all the bad karmic results! There is a way to erase some of our negative karma—purification. This requires understanding that you have behaved badly in the past and that you must take full responsibility for this behavior. Then you must sincerely regret and repent your negative actions and promise yourself to try not to behave badly again. Finally, try to perform only positive, virtuous actions from now on.

Just as musical talent may be the karmic result of musical training in an earlier life, behavioral patterns can also be karmic results. For example, if someone gets angry easily, this may be seen as a karmic consequence of previous angry behavior that the person now has the opportunity to purify. The person needs to try hard not to give in to the impulse to be angry, by reflecting that anger will create more negative karma and further intensify the habit of growing angry. While not easy, this is definitely worth attempting in order to avoid harming oneself and others in the present and in future lives.

That is a very brief introduction to karma. The following chapters examine in greater depth how karma operates and affects our lives. Practical suggestions and advice on how to generate good karma and avoid bad karma, will be offered, along with some inspiring quotations.

Once the profound nature
of karma is properly understood,
a path that can lead
to a happier life
may be discovered.

karma path to awakening

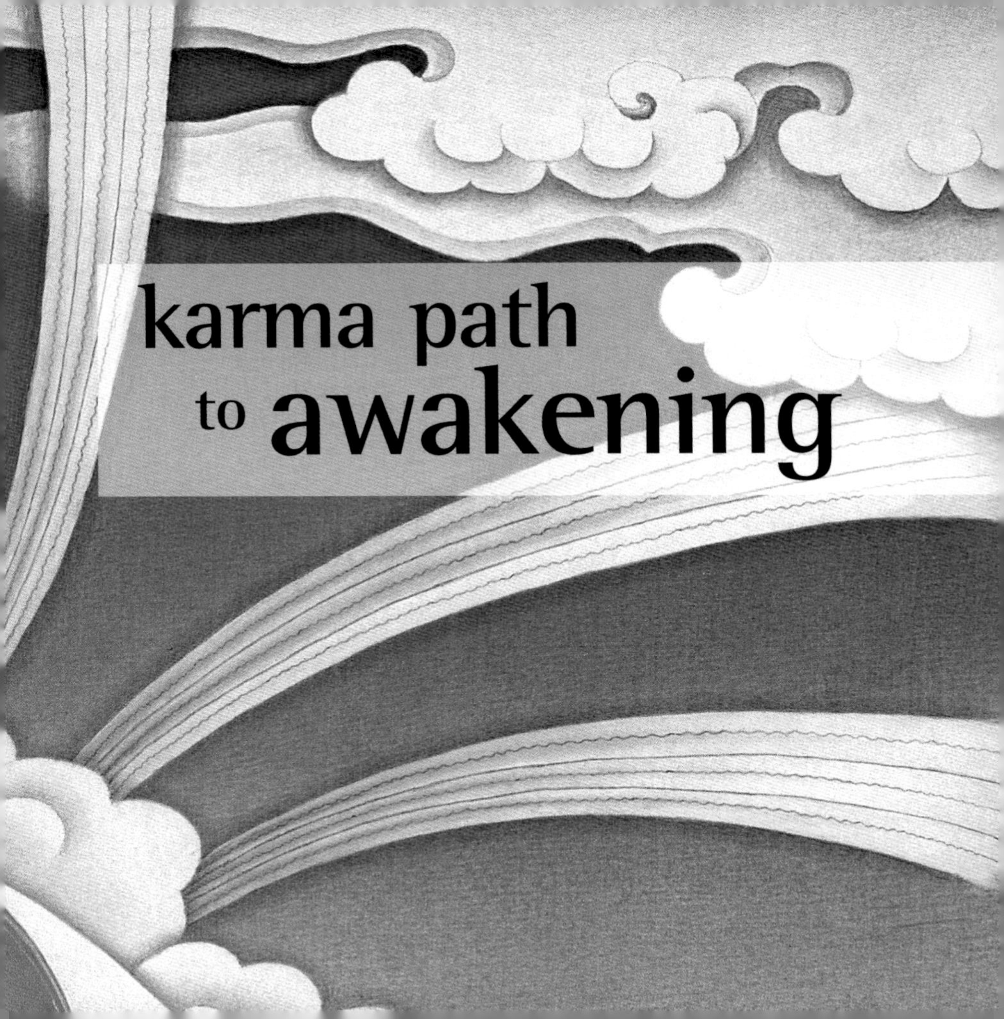

Understanding how karma operates is the key to transforming our lives, and transforming our lives is the key to discovering real happiness by awakening to our true nature. In this book you can learn about how to transform your behavior in a way that creates happiness and avoids suffering. Problems inevitably arise during the course of life; this is simply the nature of life itself.

So you can't stop problems from happening, but you can learn new, more effective ways of dealing with them.

AMITAYUS

Amitayus—meaning "Infinite Life," is the red Bodhisattva of longevity. He is seated in meditation posture with his hands holding a golden flask containing the nectar of immortal wisdom.

By being more flexible about your
attitudes toward life's difficulties
and staying open to new ideas,
you can discover ways to transform
your whole way of thinking, and
therefore transform your karma.
This is an important stage on
the path to awakening.

Awakening to your true nature does not mean
learning something new, or adopting a new

philosophy. Awakening is the inner process of letting go of habitual mistaken views, a dissolving of mental concepts, until your true nature is revealed. It is the total abandonment of ignorance, hatred, anger, desire, attachment, and aversion. This is why understanding how karma operates is fundamental to the path of awakening. Once you know that your thoughts, intentions, and actions condition your experience, then you also know that you are responsible for your own happiness and suffering. Accepting responsibility for your actions is a fundamental step toward awakening.

Awakening is also referred to as enlightenment, liberation, or nirvana. However, awakening is the most appropriate word to describe this elusive state that the Buddha experienced, because *budh*—the root of the word Buddha—means to awaken. Awakening is not only difficult to describe, but is difficult to experience. Awakening may often take many lifetimes of dedicated practice and meditation, but it is not impossible. The Buddha's life shows a living example of an awakened one, and a brief look at his life story reveals to us the authentic path to awakening, and is an inspiration to follow this for ourselves.

The life of the Buddha

The Prince Siddhartha was born about 2,500 years ago into a royal family in northern India. At the ceremony celebrating his birth a famous soothsayer, called Asita, predicted he would either be a great king or a great religious leader. This revelation greatly concerned the king who wished for his son to follow in his footsteps, and become king after his death. So the king decided his son would not have any opportunities for spiritual inquiry by confining Siddhartha to the palace and keeping him occupied with pleasure and satisfying his desires.

Siddhartha's early years were spent surrounded by luxury and beauty, with his every wish granted as soon as it was known. One day, bored with pleasure, he realized he had never stepped outside the palace walls, and wondered about the world beyond his life of luxurious confinement. The king reluctantly arranged for Siddhartha to visit the local town, but ordered his servants to keep the unpleasant facts of life away from the prince. Despite these precautions, Siddhartha saw an old person, a sick person, and a corpse. These sights troubled him greatly, as he realized that all beings,

AVALOKITESHVARA

Detail of a painting of Four-armed Avalokiteshvara, the Bodhisattva of compassion, showing his legs crossed in vajra posture above a moon disc and lotus.

including himself, would inevitably experience the pains and sorrows of old age, sickness, and death.

The way out of suffering

Feeling despondent, Siddhartha wandered down to the river to reflect on this awful new discovery. On the way he saw a holy man, wearing only rags and with few possessions, but radiating immense happiness and inner peace. Siddhartha then realized there was a way out of the suffering of existence he had just witnessed, and he resolved to leave home and learn from the great spiritual teachers of the day. He fled the palace that night, and joined the wandering holy men, studying with various spiritual masters and learning about meditation and religious philosophy. After many years of diligent meditation and practicing the ascetic's life of austerity, Siddhartha realized he had learned many beneficial spiritual techniques, but he had not yet resolved the issue of the suffering of the human condition. He sat down under a tree to meditate, and resolved not to get up until he had awakened.

For seven days Siddhartha sat in deep meditation and experienced the arising of fear and desire, but by seeing them as transitory

illusions and distractions he remained unmoved and steadfast in meditation. On the dawn of the eighth day as the light of the morning star filtered through the leaves he finally reached awakening. He had become the Buddha and realized the Four Noble Truths: that suffering exists, that the cause of suffering is craving, that there is an end to suffering, and that there is a path that leads to the end of suffering and toward awakening. The Buddha had gone completely beyond ignorance, desire, and hatred, the causes of dissatisfaction and suffering.

AURA WITH ACACIA TREE, CLOUDS, WATER, AND ROCKS

Detail of a painting of Green Tara of the acacia forest (Khadiravani Tara), showing an acacia tree branching above her aura and landscape background.

The Buddha spent the rest of his life as a simple, mendicant monk living by the principles of wisdom and compassion, and teaching the many people who were drawn toward him. Many of these people renounced everything, took ordination as monks and nuns, and joined him in the homeless life. He essentially taught meditation, morality, compassion, and wisdom—the path to extinguishing suffering and discovering happiness. He also taught his disciples about karma, the importance of recognizing that their own actions brought suffering or happiness depending on their motivation.

So what is the relevance of the Buddha's life story in a contemporary context? How can the life of an Indian holy man who lived so long ago be of benefit in our modern lives today? The Buddha was an ordinary human being, just like you and me, and just as the Buddha finally awakened to his true nature so we all have the same potential. This potential is called Buddha nature, and everyone, even animals, have Buddha nature and can eventually awaken. But we need to create the positive causes, the good karma, to be reborn as a human and live a life where we have sufficient material necessities such as food and a home, together with intelligence and the good fortune to hear about the possibility of awakening.

Following the path to awakening

Everyone reading this book has already created the good karma to have the opportunity to progress on the path to awakening. But in order to actually awaken we must put into practice the essential teachings of meditation and morality and cultivate wisdom and compassion. To protect the good karma we have now and to create more positive karma in order to be able to continue on the path to awakening we need to act wisely and compassionately. Our actions must be skillful and be motivated by altruism, and when we act we need to consider ourselves as no more important than anyone else. This can be as simple as offering our friend the largest slice of cake, or as important as saving someone from great danger.

Here's a good example. In a previous life—before the life in which he awakened—the man who would become Buddha was wandering through a forest. He encountered a starving tigress with her cubs. The poor tigress was desperate, but unable, to feed her cubs, and so weak that when she tried to attack the man she was incapable of savaging him. Overwhelmed with compassion, the man lay down and offered his own flesh to the tigress so she could feed herself and her cubs. In so doing he sacrificed his own life to be of benefit to others.

This story does not mean you should try this out for yourself! But it does show that the man—who was near awakening—had such strong compassion that he was able to give up his life without self-concern. Through the accumulation of his altruistic and skillful actions he created the good karma to be reborn as Prince Siddhartha, who

TIGER PROWLING ACROSS A TURBULENT LANDSCAPE

Detail of a painting of Dorje Drolo, one of the wrathful manifestations of Padmasambhava, who rides a tiger across an ocean of blood and wind.

eventually became Buddha. So this tale is an inspiration to start following the path to awakening, each according to her or his ability. We must be realistic about how compassionate we can be without ending up feeling hurt or resentful. However, most of us can try harder and be a little more compassionate toward others than we think we can. This creates the positive karma to continue on the path to awakening.

Cooling the passion of craving

Awakening is letting go of all desires, cravings, and wishes that things were different. It is like pulling apart veils one by one till we finally realize the peace and happiness beyond passion. In pictures where the Buddha is shown to have awakened, he is often depicted pointing to the moon, a symbol of coolness and tranquillity. Awakening can be described as cooling the passion of craving. It might not sound like much fun, because we mistakenly believe if we get what we crave then we will be happy. Awakening is the realization that there will always be something else to crave—which is a state of perpetual unfulfillment that is suffering—so abandoning craving altogether is the true path to happiness.

Sometimes awakening is thought to be a blinding flash of mystical transcendence, one magical moment and you are awakened forever. This is not so. Some people have moments of sudden realization, and the Zen tradition of Buddhism cultivates such moments, but life carries on in the same way. Such people need to deepen their experience in meditation, and must remain humble, not becoming arrogant by thinking they are better than anyone else. Most importantly they must remain mindful of their actions, and continue to act altruistically with

THE MAHASIDDHA LUIPA

Detail of a painting of Indian Mahasiddha Luipa, who was instructed by his female guru to eat fish entrails in order to overcome his discriminating pride.

wisdom and compassion and create further good karma. However, a flash of deep insight is often the inspiration to take seriously the path to awakening. If such a flash of intuitive wisdom occurs, be grateful for the insight, but do not confuse it with full awakening.

Awakening: an inner realization

The awakened ones do not turn their backs on the world. They have realized that we all live interdependently with each other and the environment, that we are intimately connected with each other and all of life. Those who have awakened live in the midst of the world, to respond to the needs of others with wisdom and compassion. They often live simple lives with few possessions, yet radiate contentment. Their many acts of kindness seem so ordinary that the recipient often doesn't notice, and they seek no recognition of their generosity, or reward.

Those who have truly awakened have gone beyond karma altogether, so there is not even the desire to create good karma from their acts of compassion; it is simply their natural response to others.

Awakening is not something to attain, it is an inner realization, and the cessation of craving. Although awakening can take many lifetimes, when the moment comes you realize that Buddha nature was there all along; you simply did not realize it. The ninth-century Chinese master Huang-po described this: "When at last in a single flash you attain full realization, you will only be realizing the Buddha nature that has been with you all the time." It is recorded that when the moment of awakening occurs the person often laughs because it now seems so obvious; life itself

VAJRA-VARAHI

Detail of a painting of the goddess Vajra-Varahi, the "adamantine sow," depicting her semiwrathful form and the sow's head that protrudes above her right ear.

has not changed, but it is now seen in a different, awakened way.

The Buddha awakened many years ago, but his teachings to help others awaken and be free from suffering have passed down to the modern day. We are fortunate to have access to his teachings and can put them into practice ourselves. There are several different Buddhist traditions, but their essential message is the same. The teachings on karma can help us take the first steps on the path to awakening. Continually reminding ourselves that our actions create karma according to the intention helps us be mindful of our actions. We know that bad actions motivated by selfishness, anger, hatred, and craving will produce bad karma and keep us trapped in suffering.

Good actions
motivated by altruism,
compassion, and wisdom
create good karma
and happiness,
and lead us down the path
to awakening.

confidence

We need to develop confidence
in our innate qualities and believe that
these can be brought to fruition.
We all have Buddha nature.

Tenzin Palmo

THE WISH-GRANTING GEM

Detail of a painting of the wish-fulfilling tree, showing the
flaming and faceted wish-granting gem amid the splendor
of the tree's flowers and foliage.

Believing in our potential to make positive changes in our lives is important. We need to have the confidence to look at our behavior, lifestyle, and thoughts and the courage to make changes to follow the path to awakening. Being prepared to make positive changes in our lives gives us the potential to transform our negative karma. Remember that you too—alongside all other living beings—have Buddha nature, the potential to awaken to your true self.

When you have good, strong self-confidence, you are less likely to feel undermined by others, or

TANTRIC STAFF (KHATVANGA)

Detail of Vajrayogini's fiery aura showing the top of her highly symbolic tantric staff, with its white ribbon, crossed vajra, golden flask, severed red head, decaying blue head, dry white skull, and surmounting trident.

need to seek their permission or authority before you act. This means that you rely on your own instincts, your inner moral guidance, and take responsibility for your actions. When this confidence and personal responsibility are reinforced by an understanding of karma, then your actions naturally tend to be positive, compassionate, and altruistic.

We all need confidence to take the first step
on the path toward awakening,
and confidence to continue when things
become difficult.

Finding a realistic sense of self

Your level of confidence depends on how you perceive yourself, and how you see yourself influences your behavior and therefore affects your karma. Avoiding the two extremes of overinflated self-importance and feelings of worthlessness promotes a balanced realistic self-perception and a confident attitude. Remind yourself that you are never as awful as you think you are when you are feeling bad, nor as great as you think you are when you are feeling good.

If you lack confidence, your actions will be uncertain. You might even end up acting from confusion and a wrong apprehension of the circumstances, and run the risk of creating mistaken karma.

Sometimes people think that if they have a mundane job—such as being a cleaner—they are not worth much. They have low self-esteem, and may not even value the work they are doing. However, many great spiritual masters of old did simple mundane work. By not identifying with the task at hand, or judging it to be lowly, they did the job as well as they could, without any negative feelings. This is confidence in action.

THE MAHASIDDHA TANTIPA

After being rejected by his family as a senile old man, Tantipa continued his tantric practice while weaving in their garden hut until he ultimately attained enlightenment.

Confidence gives courage
to inquire into
the nature of the self.

Just like everything else, the self does not have a solid inherent existence. The self depends on parents, culture, education, environment, relationships, and many other factors, thus it cannot be said to be self-existent. This can seem scary if you lack confidence and self-esteem, and this line of thinking might appear negative. However, when you feel confident it is easier to trust this beneficial line of spiritual inquiry.

Meditation exercise

Try this now, or later when you have time. Sit down and focus on your breathing for a few minutes. Then meditate on your own potential to awaken, which is definitely there because you—just like all other beings—have Buddha nature. The Buddha and other great spiritual beings have awakened already and shown the way, so it is possible. This meditation can help develop the confidence to act positively and skillfully.

Confidence and humility encourage wise and compassionate behavior.

In fact the ego is only problematic if its development has been stultified or if there is excessive clinging to it. A healthy, stable ego on the other hand, is an absolute necessity for successful functioning in the world. Without one, higher spiritual development cannot be safely undertaken and one can get stuck in all kinds of negative states, perhaps suffering much psychological pain—and certainly never fulfilling one's potential.

John Snelling

FOOT OF VAJRAYOGINI

Detail of the goddess Vajrayogini's right foot, which presses upon the breast of the red Hindu goddess Kalarati, symbolizing Vajrayogini's transcendence over desire.

Believe in your power

When we have confidence we let go of the need to control. The resulting spaciousness and flexibility influences our behavior and we are naturally kinder and more open to others, and in this way create positive karma.

Confidence helps you believe in your power and ability to accomplish your goals. Confidence also helps you define your goals with clarity, and gives you the courage to try to achieve them.

Spiritual growth is inevitably sometimes painful and difficult, but if you have the confidence to persevere then the benefits will eventually shine through. Too little confidence and you are easily manipulated by others; too much and you become arrogant. The Buddha's middle way is the best, as then you will act with sensitivity toward others and can be confident that your actions are skillful.

So, be confident—but not superior.

Having confidence and belief that the teachings on karma are worthwhile, and that they contribute to lessening suffering and increasing happiness, helps you modify your negative actions, and develop your positive actions. This helps you create less bad karma and more good karma.

Self-worth comes through appreciation
and acknowledgment of our existence,
not dependency on others. We experience
our worth as a person through knowing
ourselves, being grounded, creative,
and connected with daily life.
We learn to stop believing in the
judgmental voice from within that erodes
confidence and makes us feel inept.

Christopher Titmuss

THE OFFERING GODDESS, VAMSHA

Vamsha—the "lady of the flute," is one of the sixteen offering
goddesses who are positioned around the walls of many Buddhist
mandala palaces, four of whom play musical instruments.

Be confident enough to trust your own
inner wisdom, and courageous enough
to act on its advice.

Confidence stops you from prevaricating. It
helps you get on with living a spiritual life, acting
with wisdom and compassion, and moving
forward on the path to awakening. The confident
person acts with conviction.

Cultivate the confidence to go beyond striving
to be a better person for the sake of your own
good karma, and develop the wish to be
compassionate for the sake of all beings.

Be confident that you can free yourself from the suffering of endless rebirths by creating the positive karma to awaken. Develop confidence in your power to act with compassion.

Skeptical doubt

Buddhism teaches that there are traditionally five hindrances on the path of awakening. The fifth is skeptical doubt. Although doubt can be useful in spiritual inquiry, this specific skeptical doubt is a lack of faith, and reveals little confidence in the Buddhist teachings. The remedy for skeptical doubt is to develop confidence that the Buddhist teachings—such as karma—will lead us toward awakening, together with deepening confidence in our own abilities and spiritual aptitude.

When you are self-confident, if someone tries to undermine you in any way, you will not retaliate with anger—and create negative karma—because you are not so easily upset. You can remind yourself that the person trying to undermine you must be suffering in order to behave badly like this, and feel compassion for them.

Having the confidence to cut through what is superfluous and irrelevant is a valuable asset on the path of awakening. But following the path of awakening is not easy. The inspiration to start must be supported by the courage and confidence to continue. Meditating on karma regularly can help. By considering how you are responsible for your own actions, you realize no one else but you is in control of your behavior.

Be careful that confidence
does not turn into pride.

Wise people are confident because through their spiritual self-inquiry they have come to know their capabilities and limits. Thus they are confident in what they can and cannot do.

Self-confidence is not a form of arrogance.

It is trust in our capacity to awaken.

It is both the courage to face whatever life

throws at us without losing equanimity,

and the humility to treat every situation

we encounter as one from which

we can learn.

Stephen Batchelor

THE MAHASIDDHA NAROPA

Naropa, one of the eighty-four Mahasiddhas of ancient India
and the guru of the Tibetan translator Marpa, is depicted here
blowing upon an antelope horn.

The function of authentic spirituality
is not to provide security and solace,
but to encourage the seeker to venture out
on the lonely and difficult path
of self-knowledge.
So do not be intimidated.
Have confidence in your own
spiritual potentiality, your ability to find
your own unique way.

John Snelling

ORNATE ENLIGHTENMENT THRONE

Detail of an early painting of Green Tara, showing an upper
section of her complex enlightenment throne archway (torana)
with various sacred trees in the background.

skillful behavior

The important thing is
how we respond to our situation.
We can transform anything
if we respond in a skillful way.
This is precisely what karma is about.

Tenzin Palmo

ROCKS AND LEAVES

Detail of a painting of the Mahasiddha Naropa, showing part of
the vajra-rock formation upon which he is seated.

After the Buddha had awakened he taught the Four Noble Truths: that suffering exists, that it has a cause, that there is liberation from suffering, and that there is a path of awakening that leads to freedom from suffering. This path is called the Noble Eightfold Path.

Right Action is the fourth point on the path, and is concerned with developing skillful behavior and avoiding unskillful behavior. Right Action incorporates five precepts that we can follow to help prevent creating negative karma. The five precepts are our spiritual guides on the path of awakening. They are: not killing, not stealing, not over-indulging the senses (such as eating too much), not lying, and not abusing intoxicants.

Skillful behavior is about behaving consciously in ways that do not hurt others, and trying to be of benefit to them. Skillful behavior is wisdom in action. It is the opposite of aggressive, reactionary behavior which only perpetuates a cycle of suffering and much negative karma.

We need to learn how to be skillful in situations where there is potential for creating negative karma. If we are dealing with someone who is angry for example, we need to know how to behave so as not to aggravate the person further.

Remaining calm and not becoming angry ourselves is a skillful way of dealing with the situation, and also prevents us from accumulating the negative karmic consequences of expressing anger ourselves. Cultivating skillful behavior in this way helps us follow the path to awakening.

Skillful behavior arises from good intention. Without positive intention, your actions will be based on desire and attachment, and only lead to suffering and bad karma. When good intentions guide your actions, then this is skillful behavior that will lead to peace and happiness. Ask yourself before you act: Is this action arising from clarity or confusion? Only actions that are the result of clear motivation and intention are skillful behavior. Avoid actions that arise from a confused and turbulent mind as they only cause negative karma.

Abandoning negative feelings

In order for behavior to be skillful it is necessary to abandon negative feelings such as greed, cruelty, and craving. Suppressing these negative feelings doesn't work—they only pop up again and again—so we must consciously renounce them, by meditating on the fact that negativities cause suffering, now and in the future.

All behavior can be skillful behavior if it is done mindfully with good intentions.

Even simple, everyday tasks can be skillful behavior. The next time you wash the dishes, think about skillful behavior. This means having a good attitude and not resenting the action, not thinking, "I don't want to do the dishes. I'd much rather watch television instead." Just accept that this is what you are doing right now and by not resenting it, you can find some aspect of the task that is enjoyable, such as the satisfaction at having accomplished it well.

Not fighting and pushing for the last seat on the bus is skillful behavior. Rejoice that you have allowed someone else the opportunity to rest, and then reflect that your kind action will create positive karma.

By changing your attitude,
your mindset, into a positive one
you will experience
less dissatisfaction and can
even find happiness.
Try it and see!

The world is a place of preparation
where one is given many lessons
and passes many tests.
Choose less over more in it.
Be satisfied with what you have,
even if it is less than what others have.
In fact, prefer to have less.

Ibn'Arabi

RED PADMAPANI AVALOKITESHVARA

Detail of red Padmapani, the "lotus-bearing" Bodhisattva of
compassion who holds the stem of an immaculate white lotus.
Within his aura are depicted many mythological creatures.

Choosing to have few possessions and living a life of simplicity is fundamental to skillful behavior because it prevents greed and attachment from arising.

Choosing less over more stops negative actions of obsessional acquisitiveness, and liberates us from craving, a powerful step forward on the path to awakening.

Mindfulness before action is a helpful reminder of checking that your motivation is altruistic. Mindfulness is the precursor for skillful behavior.

HAND HOLDING ROSARY

Detail of a painting of Four-armed Avalokiteshvara, showing his uparaised second right hand holding a rosary of crystal beads as a symbol of his pure equanimity.

Skillful behavior creates good karma
and happiness. Unskillful behavior creates
bad karma and misery.

Practicing right speech

The third point on the Buddha's Noble Eightfold
Path is Right Speech, which is also part of skillful
behavior. If you speak angrily and hurt someone,
not only does it create suffering for the person at
the time, but also creates negative karma and
future suffering for yourself. Practicing Right
Speech means abandoning speech that is hurtful,
untrue, or simply a waste of time. Always think

before you speak and before you act. In this way you can check your motivation and relinquish mistaken behavior and cultivate skillful behavior.

We all have the potential to behave skillfully, and follow the path of awakening. All it takes is mindfulness and effort.

All intentional actions make karma, whether this is good or bad, because actions are based on motivation. Therefore we create our future suffering or happiness through our actions. This is why skillful behavior is so important, because it determines our future happiness, and helps us avoid suffering.

Knowing when to act and when to refrain from action is an important aspect of skillful behavior. Actions that are beneficial should be cultivated, while actions motivated by desire, anger, and ignorance are to be relinquished. There are also situations when not doing anything—even something skillful—is the best response to the circumstances. This is skillful nonbehavior.

Skillful behavior is cultivated by meditating on karma with focused concentration.

Mindful motivation behind action is more than the simple urge or impulse to act, which is without discrimination and can therefore lead to unskillful behavior. Thinking about the future results of your actions before you undertake them allows you to be selective and only act from altruism, insight, and wisdom.

Responding to dissatisfaction

Skillful behavior in response to dissatisfaction stops it from becoming anguish. For example, you see an impossibly expensive item, and desire for this object that you can never afford arises in your mind. This turns into suffering when you keep thinking about having this object, planning all sorts of ways of getting it, and yet have to keep facing the reality that it will not be yours. Skillful behavior is to observe the desire, acknowledge it has arisen, and then determine to let it go by meditating on the object's impermanence and the fact there is nothing intrinsic to the object that can make you happy. In this way, although skillful behavior cannot prevent desire from arising, it can stop it from becoming suffering.

When things don't go your way, observe your reactions. If you remain attached to the bad day you are having, keep thinking about it, complaining, and even behaving badly in response, then all you are doing is creating bad karma. Accept that today things are just not working out for you, and then reflect that you are experiencing the bad karma you previously created, and that by not reacting badly this will finish. This is skillful behavior in the face of adversity.

When you know that a certain behavioral pattern creates suffering, abandon it. Why keep on with actions that only bring misery? Strong mindfulness and determination in the face of habitual tendencies is using skillful behavior to break free from negative habits. You can do it, if you are prepared to try.

Wherever, whoever we are, all of us
are performing some actions.
We can check whether they are
beneficial for others and ourselves. . . .
The main reason for doing something
is because it is needed at that time
and one can fulfill a purpose.

Ayya Khema

HANDS OF RED GANAPATI

Detail of a painting of twelve-armed red Ganapati, the elephant-
headed "remover of obstacles," showing five of his left hands
holding a bow, khatvanga staff, skull-cup, spear, and pestle.

All actions that arise from altruism, compassion, and wisdom are skillful behavior, and can only lead to good karma and future happiness.

Cultivating these positive skillful actions is part of the path of awakening.

Devising effective ways to translate your good intentions into practical actions is a good way to develop skillful behavior. If the positive intention simply remains a thought, it is not going to be of much benefit to others, and will cause only a small amount of positive karma to arise for yourself.

GREEN TARA

The resplendent goddess of mercy and compassion, who sits in the posture of royal-ease upon a lotus throne, with her right hand held in the gesture of generosity and her left hand holding the stem of an immaculate lotus.

Out of pungent seeds

pungent fruits are born;

Out of sweet seeds, sweet fruits.

By this example, the wise should know

The bitter result of evil deeds and

The sweet result of good ones.

Suratapariprichasutra

LANDSCAPE WITH FRUIT AND TREE

Detail of a painting of a Bodhisattva, with clouds, rocks, an
entwined tree, and a stem bearing three fruits as a symbol of
the "Three Jewels" of the Buddha, dharma, and sangha.

morality

The practice of morality—guarding your three doors of body, speech, and mind from indulging in unwholesome activities—equips you with mindfulness and conscientiousness. These two factors help you avoid gross forms of negative, physical, and verbal actions, deeds that are destructive for both oneself and others.

Dalai Lama

GUARDIAN LION

Detail of a painting of Avalokiteshvara showing a mythical guardian lion, with a bell around its neck, a jewel upon its crown, and stylized mane, fur, and tail.

It is easy to take morality and ethics for granted, however, and assume we are already behaving according to our own ethical code. This can be a convenient way of choosing what we like, when we like, from a range of different philosophies. Morality according to Buddhism is an ethical code based on finding happiness and avoiding suffering for all living beings. Developing mindful awareness at all times that our behavior is indeed following a moral course of action is an important part of the path to awakening, and helps us create good karma.

JAMBHALA, THE GOD OF WEALTH

Detail of a painting of three of the five main forms of the wealth god Jambhala, with blue Jambhala represented in union with his consort at the center, white Jambhala (lower left), and black Jambhala (lower right).

Acting in an ethical manner is not always easy. It is helpful, therefore, to meditate on karma, which reminds us of how actions produce results accordingly: that good actions produce happiness and bad actions produce suffering. Remember to practice morality in daily life to take the meditation on karma beyond the theoretical and into the practical sphere.

Practicing morality is mindfully refraining from any negative actions of body, speech, and mind. When you sincerely try to avoid any negative actions, you notice that your mind becomes calm and clear, and so you feel happy. Even if you tried but did not succeed in avoiding a negative action, the karmic consequence will be much less than if you had intended it.

Everyone wants to experience happiness and avoid suffering equally. This is an inspiration to extend goodwill to everyone you meet, and behave in an ethical manner toward them.

Morality is an indispensable feature
of the path to awakening.
Therefore, it is impossible to follow the
path of awakening without morality.

Any action that is willed, however subtly, by the person who performs it will always produce a future "ripening" and ultimately a "fruit" of similar moral quality, because in the human sphere karma operates in an ethical manner.

John Snelling

FRUITS OF THE WISH-FULFILLING TREE

Detail of a painting of the divine tree of the gods, showing clusters of three fruits, rainbow emanating lotuses, hanging silk valances, and jewel chains.

Practicing morality brings happiness

We have all experienced how angry and troubled we feel—sometimes long after the event itself—if we have harmed someone, even if we felt justified and self-righteous about our behavior at the time. This is the karmic result of suffering from the negative action.

Conversely, we all know the feelings of happiness and satisfaction that arise naturally when we have helped someone. The practice of morality therefore brings immediate karmic results of happiness as well as creating positive karma that will ripen later.

Don't just think of your good points
and feel satisfied;
remember your faults as well
and try to correct them.

Morality is not about being "holier than thou," becoming a pious do-gooder with rigidly held views—despite good intentions to act ethically. We must be careful not to reduce morality to a set of inflexible rules. Morality is more of a heartfelt response to suffering supported by understanding karmic cause and effect. In other words, we naturally tend toward moral action because we see this is the best way to find happiness for ourselves and others, and to avoid suffering.

Morality includes cultivating good qualities such as kindness, wisdom, and compassion alongside refraining from negative actions. This means actively creating positive karma and avoiding negative karma. In contemporary Western culture morality has become unfashionable, and it seems fun to break the rules. But true morality as practiced in a vibrant living spiritual tradition, such as Buddhism, is not about blindly following rules. It's about discovering for ourselves what actions produce happiness and which cause suffering. Morality is about being mindful and aware, following the path of awakening, and responding to each unique set of circumstances with wisdom, compassion—and true morality.

Humans are essentially and naturally moral beings. It is only when social conditions are sufficiently poor for this natural morality to be stunted and not develop that deviant behavior arises. Humans have the impulse to act ethically, partly because a human life is the result of previous positive karma, and offers the potential to awaken. Those people who live and act in purely moral ways are seen as being noble and just. They inspire us to be more ethical ourselves. Such people provide powerful role models whose behavior we can try to emulate.

The philosophy of harmlessness

The ancient Indian philosophy of ahimsa means being harmless, not harming self, or others, or the environment we all share. This principle is the underlying basis of morality, and means we refrain from causing harm through our actions. We are all equally morally responsible for the world and everything in it.

If you do something unwittingly, or by mistake, that causes harm, the karmic consequences are much less than if you cause harm deliberately.

The aim of an awakened life is to diminish suffering. So because you care about your suffering and the suffering of others, and you understand that your intentions and actions produce consequences, you refrain from knowingly causing suffering. You try to think, speak, and act with clarity, wisdom, compassion, and respect for others.

All religions prohibit killing, because it is unethical to take the life of another being. But often we think not killing just means not killing another human being. Reflect that all beings have the right to live and to try to find happiness and avoid suffering. So next time you see a harmless insect, don't squash it mindlessly. Allow it to live its little life as part of the whole fabric of the world. You can also reflect on what you eat and try to minimize the death of animals in order to feed yourself. Even if you don't feel that you could become vegetarian, you can perhaps try to not always eat so much meat. Cultivating this harmless attitude creates positive karma.

MYTHOLOGICAL SEA-DRAGON (MAKARA)

The makara or water-monster is a hybrid animal composed of various creatures, and is often identified with the crocodile as a symbol of tenacity and power.

Ideally, ethics should spring naturally
from the heart, but in the first instance,
at the beginner's stage,
most of us need some kind of code
to guide us, though it is always more
important to keep to the spirit rather
than the letter.

John Snelling

YANTRAS

A yantra is a geometric mandala diagram, which is specifically
employed in the worship of Hindu and Jain tantric deities.
Depicted here are the yantras of nine Hindu goddesses.

Ethics provide the foundation
of a meditative life;
meditation leads to the blossoming
of wisdom, and wisdom contributes
to a more caring and ethical attitude.

Martine Batchelor

CLOUDS AND LOTUSES

Detail of a painting showing colored clouds drifting above the
lotuses around the deity's aura.

The point of morality is not to force you to blindly adhere to inflexible rules of right and wrong, but to make you reflect on your intentions and actions. In this way morality helps you create positive karma through skillful actions, and avoid karmic results from mistaken actions.

Every action, however, small or subtle, affects the entire universe.

Try to think in this way before you act, of how your actions will affect not just yourself, or those close by, but of the infinitesimal tiny reverberations your action will inevitably produce.

A morality tale

A great Zen master had a disciple who was overly obsessed with morality. The disciple's every action was considered in such minute detail before it was done that he lost all spontaneity, and no longer acted spontaneously to help others. The Zen master decided to free the disciple from his obsession in a typically Zen way. He asked the disciple to accompany him to town to do some errands. They stopped in a cafe to have something to eat, and the master ordered one vegetarian meal and one containing meat. The disciple was so fanatically vegetarian, he had forgotten the underlying kindness of refraining from eating meat in his obsession to avoid it. When the meals arrived the master gave the disciple the meat meal and ate the vegetarian meal himself.

No one is so special or clever
that they are beyond morality.
Because we are all subject
to the law of karma,
we must all try to practice morality
as much as possible.

On the Buddhist path of awakening there are three principles that are like a pyramid containing the essence of the whole path. These are morality, meditation, and wisdom. They work inter-dependently with each other, and together contribute to an awakened life.

Be realistic

You cannot expect to attain absolute moral purity very quickly; this takes time and practice. So be realistic, and don't set yourself such impossibly high standards that you will only feel disappointed when you find you can't live up to them. Start with the basic morality of not harming others or yourself through any of your actions of body, speech, or mind.

Moral certainty is an inadequate response to an ever-changing world composed of unique moments. All we can do on the path of awakening is be open to the situation with integrity and compassion. Act from the heart, not according to a set of rules, but guided by them.

Thinking about being moral
is a good start, but acting ethically
is even better.

When we consider ourselves the same as the others, everyone seeking happiness and trying to avoid suffering, then empathy naturally arises. When we truly feel empathy with others, it becomes almost impossible to act in ways that harm them. In fact, our motivation to act altruistically to help others is strengthened by reflecting on the equality of self with others.

If you do not act with morality
you are only causing
yourself future suffering
by creating negative karma.

To summarize,
when we engage in
the practice of morality,
we lay the foundation for
mental and spiritual development.

Dalai Lama

LOTUS THRONE WITH FOLIAGE

Detail of the edge of a deity's multicolored lotus throne, with
lotus blossoms, leaves, bushes, water, and rocks in the background.

changing
bad habits

This emptiness is not pure nothingness,
of course; nor is it a kind of
transcendental something.
Rather it is a medicine to remedy the
compulsive illusion-making habits of our
minds, particularly their tendency to think
of persons and things as separate,
self-created, and self-sustaining.

John Snelling

SILK SCARVES WITH CLOUDS AND RAINBOW

Detail of a painting of the Mahasiddha Ghantapa, showing part
of the multicolored brocade scarves worn by Ghantapa and his
consort as they fly in union through the sky.

When we meditate on emptiness, the lack of inherent existence of all things and people, our rigid views of how things exist dissolve. We realize the potential in every moment as an opportunity to act differently. Understanding emptiness and using it to overcome habitual negative actions is an important part of the path to awakening.

Humans are creatures of habits, and sadly most of these are not good! Obviously damaging habits—such as smoking cigarettes that endanger health—are clear to see, even if the addiction is

WHITE TARA

The goddess of love and compassion, with the three eyes in her face symbolizing the purity of her body, speech, and mind, and the four eyes in her palms and soles the "four immeasurables" of compassion, love, sympathetic joy, and equanimity.

hard to give up. However, there are many less obvious bad habits such as habitually reacting in negative ways when things go wrong in daily life. Habitual behavior stops us thinking about what it is we are doing as we mindlessly follow our habit. Being conscious of our behavior at all times helps us change our bad habits, and our karma.

You need to be aware of your bad habits. Only when you are aware of your bad habits and have an understanding of them can you work at changing them.

Reflecting on the consequences of habitual bad actions can be a strong inspiration to abandon them. For example, the consequences of being habitually greedy and always eating too much include obesity, feelings of lack of self-worth, and health problems. Greed often encourages other bad habits such as selfishness, which manifests in negative actions like always grabbing the last cookie before someone else has had a chance. When someone knows that greed is one of their bad habits, reflecting on the various consequences can help them overcome their habitual tendencies, and steer them toward more positive behavior.

If we don't change
our minds and our actions,
if we don't stop creating negative karma,
there will always be
more negativity to purify.

Lama Zopa

DRAGON WITH CLOUDS, LOTUSES, AND RAINBOW

Detail of a painting of Four-armed Avalokiteshvara, showing an azure dragon
amidst clouds, and part of the deity's rainbow aura with lotuses.

Meditation exercise

Meditation is a powerful medicine for the poison of bad habits. After sitting watching your breath come and go for a few minutes, allow thoughts of craving and other bad habits to surface in your mind. Look at each one. Notice how the impulse to action arises. Observe it, let it be. Eventually it will pass into cessation in the same way of all thoughts and emotions. The negative karma of repeating yet again a habitual negative action has been skillfully avoided this time, and through repeated meditation practice the impulse to action will lessen and eventually cease altogether.

Major bad habits

There are deeply ingrained bad habits that almost everyone shares that are the result of habitual behavior over many different lifetimes. These include the tendency to always be wanting something: new possessions, for circumstances to be different, to be prettier, richer, have more time, and so on. These are the major bad habits of desire, and aversion—the craving for things to be other than they are. How do you work with trying to change the bad habits of many lifetimes? You start slowly without expectations of changing these habits quickly. But you do make a start, by

observing craving arise and trying to let it go as soon as you notice you are caught up in it. Don't try to manipulate life; let things be as they are.

We can find the inspiration to let go of craving for things to be different in our own modern culture as well as in the Buddhist teachings. For example, the Beatles sang, "Speaking words of wisdom, let it be, let it be." We can use this wonderful and catchy phrase as a modern mantra, something we can repeat a few times every time we catch ourselves caught up in craving. Let it be.

VAJRAYOGINI

The red Highest Yoga Tantra goddess in her form as Naro Khajoma, gazing upward while drinking from a skull-cup of blood, her right hand circling a knife downward and a tantric staff (khatvanga) resting across her left shoulder.

Transforming bad habits into mindful, altruistic actions is the essence of karma.

To walk the path of awakening is to respond to circumstances with wisdom and compassion. Therefore the task is to free the mind from the impulse toward habitual negative behavior, because such blind, unthinking actions prevent us from being wise and compassionate in response to our circumstances.

Meditating on our interdependence with everyone else and the environment helps reduce selfishness, the mind that considers oneself as more important than anyone else. As most bad habits arise from narrow-minded self-concern, thinking about the needs of others as equal to your own helps transform habitual negative action and the resultant negative karma.

Each time you confront

a habitual bad action,

you are creating the possibility

for change.

Free yourself from your bad habits!

Compulsive behavior

What is a bad habit? It is any compulsive and often repeated action that causes suffering and creates negative karma. Furthermore, although we think our bad habits only affect ourselves adversely, they may well cause suffering to others. As an example, we only need to think of smoking, and the damage from passive smoking to those other people around the person actually smoking the cigarette.

Ask yourself, "Do I really want to keep on suffering through endlessly repeating my bad habits? Or do I want to try to break free from them, by meditating on the karmic consequences of my negative behavior and practicing being mindful so I don't act out the impulse when it arises in my mind?"

At the moment your bad habits are in charge; your actions are controlled by them. Resolve to take hold of the reins of your actions and transform your negative habits.

Not acting out our bad habits

gives us the opportunity to try

something different.

Imagine being at the receiving end of one of your bad habits, such as having to put up with your own habitual chattering about if only life were different. Seeing your bad habits through the eyes of someone else can be a powerful impulse to change.

Understanding that your bad habits are negative actions that will create bad karma gives you the wisdom to be able to change them. Accepting that you have bad habits and being familiar with them is a good start to abandoning them. However, if understanding does not lead to the relinquishing of bad habits, then it is not much use.

You are not your bad habits

Don't be the victim of your bad habits, and the bad karma they create. Take control of your life and your actions by reflecting on karma, and the unfortunate consequences of suffering caused by your bad habits. If you identify with your bad habits as an integral part of yourself it will be much harder to want to change them. Remember that your bad habits are simply compulsive negative actions, and you can change them by mindfully restraining yourself from acting when the impulse arises. Each time you don't act out a bad habit, it weakens.

It is hard to recognize the extent of our mental habits, and it is hard to break them. But as we become more familiar with the way the mind works, then the more we see the connection between our motives, thoughts, actions, and responses. . . . Becoming aware of actions and the consequences of those actions reveals the correcting mode of karma in our lives.

Diana St. Ruth

DANCING GANESH

Detail of a painting of the white four-armed form of the elephant-headed god Ganesh, who dances upon his rat mount while holding a rosary, a white radish, an ax, and a bowl of Indian sweets known as laddu.

You have the opportunity right now
during today to decide to stop
one of your bad habits.
Take the opportunity while you can,
before your bad habits get the better of you,
and increase your negative karma.

Sometimes our bad habits seem like they are of benefit to us, so we need to check out all our habits in meditation. Inquire into the nature of the habit, check to see if the consequences bring suffering or happiness for yourself or others, see if the habitual behavior prevents you from thinking clearly. You may be surprised to find that many habits are in fact quite negative, not least because habitual behavior often prevents us from responding mindfully to each unique moment we find ourselves in.

Above all, be compassionate toward yourself. You are unlikely to be able to change all your bad habits quickly. Find a balance between being too hard on yourself and then giving up when you can't live up to your impossibly high standards, and being too soft and allowing yourself to indulge your bad habits.

You need to build the power of creative
awareness by meditating regularly.
Over time, stillness and clarity will be
developed and you will be surprised at
the habits and patterns you recognize
and are able to shed like
old, worn-out clothes.

Martine Batchelor

THE MAHASIDDHA MANIBHADRA

Manibhadra was one of only four women who are listed among the
eighty-four Mahasiddhas. For twelve years she lived as a model wife
and mother while perfecting her tantric practice, then she levitated
into the sky and was absorbed into the paradise of the dakinis.

transforming
adversity

Even if you cannot lead a single-minded life of Dharma [Buddhist] practice, it is very beneficial to reflect on these teachings as much as possible and make efforts to consider as transitory all adverse circumstances and disturbances. Like ripples in a pool, they occur and soon disappear. Insofar as our lives are karmically conditioned, they are characterized by endless cycles of problems, which arise and then subside.

Dalai Lama

AN ASSEMBLY OF OFFERINGS

Landscape detail of a lotus throne rising from a lake with an offering assembly of jewels, cymbals, a conch, a flute, and the seven possessions of a Universal Monarch or Chakravartin.

When things go wrong we tend to become depressed or angry, or feel hopeless. If instead we regard these misfortunes as opportunities for change, with wisdom and effort we can transform how we think about and deal with unfortunate circumstances. We can't stop bad things happening—they are a part of life—but we can change our responses, and develop a more skillful outlook, which in turn will transform our bad karma into positive karma.

How do you go about transforming adversity? As you cannot change the adverse circumstances themselves you are faced with transforming your strong negative feelings: the passions of anger, hatred, and aversion. As these passions are so strong, this is no easy task, but by practicing patience, moral restraint, and wisdom gradually you can change negative emotions.

Patience is our greatest friend in helping transform adversity.

You can use skillful methods to combat the powerful enemies of anger and hatred. Bringing reason and analysis into play undermines the fiery heat of these negative emotions. When anger arises as a response to an adverse situation, stop.

Think about how your anger is not helping and is in fact causing you suffering: a fast-beating pulse, pain in the heart, constricted breathing. Furthermore your anger is not improving the situation. Reflect that although anger has arisen, you don't have to act it out, you can choose to let it go. Remember that acting from anger creates powerful negative karma and future suffering. Breathe deeply and imagine your anger leaving on the out breath. In this way you help expel the anger without acting it out and thereby aggravating the already difficult situation.

TEN-ARMED VAJRA-VARAHI

She dances upon a goddess riding on a fish, with her ten hands holding a knife, ax, vajra, rosary, and drum (right); and a skull-cup, trident, book, noose, and bell (left).

It's hard to understand why a person
suffers in the way that they do.
The mind is so powerful and it controls
our body and speech.
If the mind is unhappy and confused
so much suffering can arise.

Ani Zamba

YESHE TSOGYAL

Yeshe Tsogyal was the seventh-century Tibetan princess who
became a consort of Padmasambhava and assisted him in
establishing the Buddhist teachings in Tibet.

Learning how to skillfully transform adversity is an important step on the path of awakening.

Remaining detached

An important aspect of transforming adversity is to lessen the personal feelings of attachment to the situation. This means transforming the usual view of "why did this happen to me?" It didn't. The situation arose from causes and conditions and you are only a small part of the equation. Practice detachment from the difficult situation by regarding it as just a difficult situation, not yours. A detached view allows a clearer perspective to arise so you can see what needs to be done to transform the adversity. This perspective allows you to act for the greatest good, not just for your personal advantage.

When you inquire into the nature of adverse situations, you discover that you are a part of it; it is not separate from you. Thus you are partly responsible. Acknowledging your part in the process and taking responsibility for it helps evade the helpless feeling of being victimized by difficult situations.

With proper understanding, every
experience, whether positive or negative,
can be a constructive step on the path.

Kathleen McDonald

URGYEN MENLA

Urgyen Menla is the deep blue form in which Padmasambhava manifests as the Medicine Buddha. This detail shows his left hand holding a skull-cup filled with the medicinal fruit myrobalan.

If you express negative emotions in a difficult situation, it will only make things worse, and create future suffering. However, repressing the negative emotions will also cause problems later. The best approach is to meditate on the damaging potential of acting out the negative emotion, and the suffering it will cause yourself and others. Then analyze it, until you realize that such negative feelings are mistaken. Cultivating the positive counter emotion is also of great benefit, such as cultivating patience in the face of anger.

Working with your negative emotions skillfully through meditation is the best way to transform them, and, eventually, eliminate them altogether. Keeping a balanced and happy mind in the face of adversity prevents hatred from arising. Reflect that feeling unhappy serves no purpose in overcoming the problematic situation.

The path of awakening includes finding equanimity in all situations.

When you respond to adverse circumstances with compassion and wisdom, then life itself becomes a great teacher as you stay open to learning from the troublesome episode, and create positive karma. Remember that you have human intelligence, that you can choose how you respond to adverse circumstances, and that you are responsible for your actions.

Learning from adversity

Buddha taught that we are not just here to have a good time; through our karma we are here in a human rebirth so we have the opportunity to learn from adversity and awaken to our true nature.

Try this. Imagine that someone has insulted you, and by remembering a previous real incident, recall your feelings and reactions. Really try to recall the power of your feelings at that time. Then reflect that in this imaginary scenario you have a choice. You can choose to insult the person in retaliation, you can slink off feeling humiliated and worthless, you can blame yourself, or you can respond positively by viewing the situation with understanding and patience, and not apportioning blame to anyone. This last option is skillful action that does not create negative karma.

Next time suffering arises, reflect that perhaps the adversity you are experiencing is nothing more than your craving for the circumstances to be different from what they are. If you arrive at the conclusion that it is definitely not your craving for things to be different, then reflect that this is a wonderful opportunity to use up and eliminate some of your negative karma created from an earlier unskillful action.

Transforming adversity can be as simple as thinking about it differently. Instead of feeling trapped by a difficult situation, regard it as an opportunity to break free from your habitual thought and behavioral patterns. Responding from an openness of heart free from the notion of an independently existent self is walking the path of awakening.

Might meets skillfull means

An invading army arrived in a small town ready to kill anyone who resisted them. Most people immediately surrendered or fled. The army general strode into the Zen Buddhist temple and encountered a Zen priest. Annoyed that the priest showed no fear and did not immediately fall to the ground and beg for his life, the general waved his sword menacingly and yelled, "Don't you know that you are looking at a man who could run you through without blinking?" The priest replied calmly, "And you, sir, are looking at a man who can be run through without blinking." The shocked general had no answer to this skillful reply, so he simply bowed respectfully and left.

Giving way without anger

Arguments often arise over two different points of view. Remembering that points of view have no solid existence or inherent truth, and that a point of view is simply one person's perception, helps let go of attachment to one's own point of view. The argument can then usually be resolved swiftly.

Letting the other person have their way in a dispute is a sign of strength and wisdom, not a

DISCIPLE OF THE BUDDHA

Detail of a painting of Shakyamuni Buddha showing one of his two main disciples, Maudgalyayana, who stands holding an alms-bowl and a mendicant's staff before the lion throne of the Buddha.

sign of weakness. Why is this? Giving in to the other person, letting them have their way, firstly prevents the dispute from continuing and causing further anger, hatred, and other negative emotions that create negative karma. Secondly, it shows an understanding of the ultimate emptiness of all views—even your own precious and cherished beliefs—which is a definite sign of well-developed wisdom. Lastly, recall a time when you won an argument and remember how hollow the victory seemed shortly afterward. So giving way to the other person is the best thing to do from several perspectives.

Practicing patience in the face of adversity not only prevents us from acting from anger and creating negative karma, but lessens the suffering of the undesirable situation and creates positive karma and future happiness.

An adverse situation is bad enough

without being made worse with anger.

When faced with adverse circumstances reason if anything can be done to resolve it. If resolution is possible, then there is no need to worry. However, if nothing can be done to resolve it, it is pointless to worry. Either way, worrying is a waste of time.

Meditation cannot prevent
difficult things from happening to you,
but a meditative attitude can help you
deal with them.

Martine Batchelor

FOUR-ARMED AVALOKITESHVARA

The white Bodhisattva of compassion, who holds the attributes of a rosary,
lotus, and a wish-granting gem clasped before his heart. His rainbow aura
encloses red lotus blossoms with colorful birds alighting upon them.

When you are faced with adverse circumstances, feeling unhappy serves no purpose in overcoming the undesirable situation. It is not only futile but will, in fact, serve to aggravate your own anxiety and bring about an uncomfortable and dissatisfied state of mind. . . . Rather than being unhappy and hateful, we should rejoice in the success of others.

Dalai Lama

LION SUPPORTING LOTUS THRONE

Detail of the lotus throne of Vajrasattva, which is supported by paired white lions standing upon golden crest bars. Below the throne are stacked jewels and the seven possessions of the Universal Monarch or Chakravartin.

purification

We don't have to be burdened by
the wrong things we did in the past.
We can do purification practices.

Tenzin Palmo

THE BUDDHA'S ENLIGHTENMENT THRONE

Detail of the jeweled aura and enlightenment throne of
Shakyamuni Buddha, showing a young god (deva) riding upon
a mythological creature (sharabha) while supporting a golden
crest bar with a water-dragon (makara) standing upon it.

Throughout this life and many previous lives we have accumulated a great deal of bad karma, some of which will cause an unpleasant effect in this life, and the remainder will condition our future lives adversely. However, we do have the opportunity to purify some of this bad karma in this life, here and now. If, for example, we have deliberately endangered someone—or even an animal—at some point in our lives, to purify the karma we need to offer safety and refuge from danger to other beings as much as we can.

You can think of purifying negative karma in terms of its effect on your consciousness. If you have done something you know is wrong—even a long time ago—feelings of guilt will lurk somewhere in the unconscious and cause discomfort and suffering from time to time. If you do not purify this negative karma, then it will carry over to the next rebirth.

When you first acknowledge that you have done many wrong actions throughout your life, it is easy to fall into the trap of low self-esteem. You can end up feeling everything is hopeless. However, you do not have to self-identify with your negative side any more than your positive side. If you start feeling depressed about your previous bad actions and their consequences, then you can recall the many positive actions you have also done. This gives a balanced perception, and avoids extreme self doubt or smug complacency.

The essence of purification is simply to let go of your problems and mistakes by seeing them as temporary blips on your stream of consciousness, not as an intrinsic part of your nature. By not identifying with your problems and mistakes, and by seeing their transitory nature, they become less difficult to deal with skillfully, and are easier to let go of and purify.

ROCKS AND SWIRLING WATER

Detail of a painting of Thousand-armed Avalokiteshvara, showing angular rock formations rising above a swirling lake, and with part of the deity's lotus throne at the upper right.

If the doors of perception
were cleansed,
every thing would appear
to man as it is,
infinite.

William Blake

THE PARADISE REALM OF AMITABHA

Detail of a painting of the pure realm of Amitabha Buddha, which
is known as Sukhavati (Tib. dewa-chen), showing three of the eight
great Bodhisattvas, four monks making offerings, the Buddha
Ratnasambhava, and beings taking "lotus-birth" within a lake.

Purification cleanses our consciousness
and transforms how we perceive
the world, revealing the true nature
of existence as a vast web of
interconnected energy.

Then we no longer view the world through the narrow prism of self-concern, and can easily see the way forward for the greatest good.

It is not just our negative actions that we purify, but the state of mind underlying the action. In other words we purify our negative thinking.

Meditation exercise

When you meditate the impulse to action arises in the mind repeatedly. These are some of the most predominant thoughts that arise in the mind during meditation. Observing these desires and then letting them go without acting them out is a skillful way to decrease their strength and lessen the grip of bad habits. This is purification of mindless habitual behavior.

The following meditation is a simple yet powerful purification practice. Spend a few minutes sitting quietly and bringing your attention to your breathing, noticing each inhalation and each exhalation. On the next exhalation, imagine all your negative energy leaves your body. Visualize the negative energy as black smoke that you breathe out into the vastness of space where it disappears completely, not adversely affecting anyone or anything. On the next inhalation visualize positive energy from the universe filling your body in the form of pure white light. It permeates every cell in your mind and body making you feel calm and happy. Practiced regularly for five to ten minutes each time, this purification meditation helps you along the path to awakening.

There is a Buddha of purification called Vajrasattva, whose body is visualized as radiant white light. He exists to help all living beings purify their negative energy and eventually awaken. The meditation practice of Vajrasattva is said to be as powerful at burning away our delusions and negative energy as a raging fire destroys thousands of acres of forest.

The path to purification

One of the laws of karma is that the result of any action increases over time in the same way one fruit seed grows into a tree and makes many fruits. This is an incentive to purify our minds so we do not commit negative actions again, as well as purifying the karma from our previous negative actions. Whenever we are tempted to put off purifying our negative actions, thinking there is no harm to leave them for a while, we can remind ourselves that the longer we leave it, the greater it will be.

Purification involves a process of simplifying our lifestyle, doing less actions, and resting content in simply being, a state of mind found in meditation. Doing less allows us to enjoy life more, because there is more space to simply be.

The karmic result of our earlier negative actions is the troubling memory left behind. The fear, anxiety, and worry that arise when the memory surfaces in consciousness are the karmic result of unenlightened behavior.

However, for purification to be effective it must be supported by understanding and acceptance. We need to understand karma, but equally we need to understand our own impulse to action and the actions, and the consequences of the actions, themselves. We need to accept what stage we are on the path to awakening, and that even when we understand that bad actions need purifying we still sometimes do them. This is simply human nature; we cannot behave perfectly just because we would like to. We do not become awakened overnight—but with daily effort and mindfulness gradually we notice small changes.

Purifying your negative actions might seem like a difficult task. So remind yourself that the aim of purification—like all genuine spiritual practice—is to bring a release from suffering, and to find peace and happiness. By genuinely regretting your previous negative actions, trying sincerely not to repeat them, and consciously making amends you can definitely purify some of your negative karma.

Cultivating positive karma

Alongside purification of the negative karma of an unskillful action we need to cultivate positive karma from a skillful action of a similar nature. Imagine a person who used to practice theft, but has now resolved to abandon such mistaken action, through seeing the unfortunate results of experiencing the negative karmic consequences. The best actions to cultivate counteractive positive karma are those of generosity and giving, and the person should practice these qualities whenever possible and even search out opportunities to give his or her possessions away.

The great Tibetan Buddhist saint Milarepa learned black magic in his youth to take revenge on behalf of his mother, who had been wronged by some relatives. He used his powers to create a storm that caused the death of several people, some birds, and the destruction of a house. Later on, Milarepa understood the gravity of his actions and their karmic consequences and wished to purify the negative karma. He searched for a spiritual master, repented, regretted, and submitted to terrible hardships that his master put him through. He also spent many years

MILAREPA

Milarepa (1040–1123) is Tibet's most beloved ascetic and yogin. He is depicted here in the posture of song in his retreat cave, with the nettles upon which he subsisted growing to his left.

meditating. In this way, Milarepa was able to purify these negative acts in the same lifetime they were committed, and eventually attained perfect awakening.

Purify your negative karma before it manifests as suffering.

Although we cannot know for certain, over many different rebirths we will have definitely committed many negative actions. But purification practices and meditations can definitely eliminate this negative karma.

Meditation exercise

The following meditation is useful for purifying specific negative actions. Watch your breath come and go for a few minutes, and bring to mind one or more negative actions you have committed in the past. Generate sincere repentance and regret for having done them, and sincerely resolve not to do these bad actions again. You can then ask the Buddha—or whichever God or spiritual source is appropriate for you—to help you keep your resolution. Then visualize the negative energy as black smoke dissipating on the next few out breaths, and spiritual strength in the form of pure white light entering your body during the next few in breaths. You can instead meditate on generating love and compassion and the power of these positive qualities to overcome negativities if you find visualization difficult.

Purification is of benefit to yourself because you learn to give up bad actions, and is of benefit to others as you start acting toward them with kindness and generosity. In this way, the purification of bad behavior is a fundamental part of the path to awakening.

Purification has only been truly effective in clearing negative karma when one's actions spontaneously manifest positive qualities such as love, wisdom, and compassion.

The purification of negative karma
causes peace of mind, a compassionate heart,
and wise behavior.

Don't put off purifying your negative karma until it's too late, and death arrives. Whatever unpurified negative karma is left from this and previous lifetimes will go forward to condition your next life adversely, and also cause difficult circumstances to arise in future lifetimes. So it is best to act now while you have the opportunity.

Purify yourself and become dust
So that from your dust
flowers can grow.

Jalaluddin Rumi

GREEN TARA

The goddess of compassion, who is seated upon a moon disc
and lotus in the posture of "royal-ease," with her right hand
making the gesture of generosity, and her left hand holding the
stem of a lotus before her heart.

Although we may have faults and problems it is wrong to think that they are permanent. We can free ourselves from negative energy and the burden of guilt, as long as we are willing to work. One way of doing this is through the process of purification.

Kathleen McDonald

RED GANAPATI

The twelve-armed red form of the elephant-headed "remover of obstacles," who dances above his rat mount within an elaborate enlightenment throne or torana.

What you do, you remember;
it's as simple as that.
If you do something kind, generous, or
compassionate, the memory makes you feel
happy; and if you do something mean and
nasty, you have to remember that.
You try to repress it, run away from it, get
caught up in all kinds of frantic behavior—
that's the kammic result.

Ajahn Sumedho

YESHE TSOGYAL

Detail of a painting of Padmasambhava with his two main
consorts. This detail shows only his Tibetan consort Yeshe
Tsogyal, while the other side of the painting would depict his
Indian consort Mandarava.

a new way
of seeing

From a Buddhist point of view,
this universe is created by
the karma of the beings within it.
So in one way we are all holding it
together ourselves.

Tenzin Palmo

NYINGMA ASSEMBLY TREE

Detail of a complex painting depicting Padmasambhava (top center) with all of the main Buddhas, Bodhisattvas, tantric deities, and protective deities of the early Nyingma tradition of Tibetan Buddhism.

We take our normal mode of perception for granted, so it can be difficult to transform. Consider the following. Water to a fish is home, to a drowning man the enemy, to the thirsty man delightful, to the physicist a collection of molecules. Is there a right and wrong perception?

Transforming how we see
things exist in the world deepens our
understanding of karma.

We tend to see things in isolation from each other, as existing independently, and especially we regard ourselves as autonomous beings. This makes it easier to act in ways that create suffering. However, when we see things as existing in dependence on causes and conditions we develop more respect for the whole web of life itself. For example, when we eat a slice of bread we can reflect that it only exists because of the farmer who grew wheat, the miller who ground flour, the baker who made bread, and the driver who delivered it to the bakery. It also took sunshine, fertile soil, and rain for the slice of bread to come into existence, so we see there are many interdependent factors involved.

To see a World in a Grain of Sand
And a Heaven in a Wild Flower,
Hold Infinity in the palm of your hand
And Eternity in an hour.

William Blake

Letting go of the illusion of independent existence and the suffering this inevitably entails is seeing clearly the path of awakening. Once you let go of the fiction of an independent self, you become aware of the vast intricate web of life as it manifests each moment. This is freedom from the narrow constraints of the ego self, and when this freedom is realized your actions spontaneously become wise and compassionate.

Seeing how the world truly exists is awakening to your true nature. When we transform our perception and see for ourselves the true nature of reality, it is like scales falling from our eyes.

Someone once asked the Buddha what he had gained from enlightenment (awakening). He replied, "I attained absolutely nothing from full and perfect enlightenment." The Buddha's answer reveals how we can transform our usual materialistic vision into a way of seeing that recognizes awakening is about losing, not gaining. We too can lose the veils of illusion.

When you practice meditation regularly, gradually you notice the mind calms down. You feel peaceful and able to let thoughts go as they arise rather than following them. You realize you don't have to think all the time. This allows the inner life—usually obscured by clouds of thoughts—to flourish, and you catch a glimpse of the nature of your mind beneath the superficial thoughts. When this quality permeates your everyday life, your actions become less self-centered and more spacious. You are more in touch with the world beyond self.

Ask yourself what is unnecessary
in your life and clear it away.
The simple, uncluttered life allows you
to see what's really important.

Cleansing perception

Training the mind through meditation cleanses perception and transforms our normal deluded ways of seeing.

The freedom from craving that awakening entails is the freedom to act for the benefit of others. Once you let go of self-centered craving, life unfolds in the here and now. You see the mystery of life and recognize the unique circumstances that make up each moment.

Responding with compassion and wisdom to what you encounter rather than acting from self-interest seems the only way to be.

We are our own jailers.
We keep ourselves unfree by clinging,
out of confusion and fear, to a self that
exists independently of all conditions.
Instead of accepting and understanding
things as they are, we seek independence
from them in the fiction of
an isolated selfhood.

Stephen Batchelor

VAJRASATTVA AND CONSORT

Detail of the white Bodhisattva of purification in sexual union
with his white consort. Vajrasattva holds the paired attributes
of a vajra and bell in his right and left hands, symbolizing the
union of his skilful method and wisdom.

The fundamental change of perception that leads to awakening is seeing the futility of desire, that it only leads to suffering and not to happiness. Seeing desire for what it really is—a recurring instrument of suffering—gives the freedom not to act from habitual craving.

Karma is the cause that results in happiness or suffering, depending on whether the intention, action, and result are positive or negative. If you meditate on this regularly, gradually your perception will evolve into an understanding of how karma operates. This way of seeing is beyond an intellectual comprehension; it means your actions naturally become motivated for the greater good, beyond self-interest.

Views don't last

We live in a world of ever-changing flux, where nothing is fixed or certain. Views come and go, and what was once taken for granted is now disproved, such as the belief that the world is flat. You would have been considered crazy to dispute this at the time it was commonly believed, crazy to believe it now. This is the emptiness of views.

When we make a concerted effort to develop our minds we make progress by transforming our way of seeing, our attitudes, and behavior. Gradually we gain insight into the profoundest subjects, such as karma, and it is eventually possible for each one of us to awaken to our true Buddha nature.

Next time you are involved in a dispute or an argument remember that it's just two, or more, people holding different views, and that these views are ultimately empty of any definitive meaning. Becoming angry and creating negative karma by shouting at the other person while you are defending your viewpoint not only causes suffering, but is pointless.

What is your most important consideration before acting? If it is personal gain, this will only cause suffering. However, if you make your most important consideration the results of your actions, then this acts as a guide on what to do and what not to do. It promotes worthwhile actions and avoids unskillful actions.

Cultivate the view that—at best—if you are able to, you should help others, but if you are not able to help others, then—at least—do not harm them.

We are innovative beings so discovering new ways of seeing—based on our understanding of karma—is a creative act of the imagination.

Therefore we know that, unawakened,
even a Buddha is a sentient being,
and that even a sentient being,
if he is awakened in an instant of
thought, is a Buddha.

Hui Neng

LOTUS BLOSSOMS, LEAVES, AND BILLOWING CLOUDS

Detail of a painting of Sarasvati, showing a pink lotus and its leaves
arising above a lake, with multicolored clouds curling behind.

Transform your perception
like a flower that freshly opens
every morning with the rising sun.

Practicing nonattachment to how we see the world allows the opportunity and space for transforming our currently limited perception. However, grasping at your own particular way of seeing can cause conflict with other people because you forget that there are other valid ways of seeing. When you are in conversation with someone who sees things differently from you, pause. Are you judging the person according to his or her view? Has your opinion become rigid so that you now think it is the only worthwhile opinion, and will fight to defend it? Instead, be open, listen to the other person's point of view—you might learn something that helps you transform your own way of seeing things.

You yourself create your reality through your actions, or in other words, the protector and destroyer of happiness are your own karma. Your own virtuous actions cause and protect happiness, while any action you take that lacks virtue causes harm and destroys your happiness.

Don't limit yourself

If you are not open to transforming your vision of the world, you are limiting yourself. Be open, nonattached and nongrasping. Allow each new experience in your life to teach you something new by trying to see it with fresh eyes, beyond your usual perception.

When you meditate, you start with watching the breath come and go, then you observe thoughts arise and pass. Once your mind has calmed and quieted, you can stop everything. Just sit there not doing anything at all, just being in the moment open to anything and everything—

sounds, smells, emotions, thoughts, sensations. Being open to everything without attachment or judgment in this meditative spaciousness allows new ways of seeing to spontaneously arise in your consciousness.

At the root of our deluded ways of seeing is the ignorance that conceives of objects and people as inherently existing. This mistaken view gives rise to afflictive emotions such as anger, hatred, pride, and jealousy. Meditating on the lack of inherent existence and the interdependent nature of all things gives rise to a new way of seeing that dispels suffering and brings happiness.

Just like a dream experience,

Whatever things I enjoy

Will become a memory.

Whatever has passed

will not be seen again.

Nagarjuna

LOTUS AND BIRD WITH BILLOWING CLOUDS

Detail of a painting of White Tara, showing a bird of paradise
resting upon a pink lotus, with finely shaded clouds billowing
in the upper sky.

About the artist

Robert Beer (born 1947), a British artist, has studied and practiced Tibetan thangka painting for more than thirty years. One of the first Westerners to become actively involved in this art form, he initially studied for a period of five years in India and Nepal with several of the finest Tibetan artists living at that time. Since 1975 he has lived in Britain and worked consistently on developing the artistic skills, vision, patience, and understanding of this highly complex subject, as well as the historical and cultural context within which it arises. His drawings and paintings have appeared in several hundred books on Tibetan Buddhist art and religion, and he is widely regarded as one of the world's leading experts on this subject. His publications include *The Encyclopedia of Tibetan Symbols and Motifs* and *The Handbook of Tibetan Buddhist Symbols*.

Over the last ten years he has been commissioning and collecting works by the finest contemporary Nepali and Tibetan artists, and he has also been instrumental in introducing the skills of Tibetan art to some of the most accomplished Indian miniature painters of Rajasthan. The paintings of many of these artists appear in this book, and include the Newar artists: Siddhimuni and Surendra Man Shakya, Udaya and Dinesh Charan Shrestha, Lalman Lama, Ajay Lama, Sundar Singhwal, Devendra Singhwal, Samundra Singhwal, Amrit Dangol, Raj Prakash, Amrit Devendra, Kungchang Lama, Ratna Bahadur and Sundar Shrestha. The Tibetan artists include Chewang Lama, Phunsok Tsering, and the studios of Cho Tsering and Dawa-la. The Rajastani artists include Babulal and Jai Shankar, both of whom have worked under the supervision of Marc Baudin of Jaipur.

With gratitude
to everyone who helped
bring this book to fruition.

Gill Farrer-Halls

Every effort has been made to obtain permission to
reproduce materials protected by copyright. Where omissions
have occurred please contact Gill Farrer-Halls,
c/o Elizabeth Puttick Literary Agency, 46 Brookfield Mansions,
Highgate, West Hill, London, N6 6AT.